Ten Facts You Should Know Before Making

THE DECISION TO MEDICATE YOUR CHILD

by Mary Ammerman, Psy.D.
Ed Hamlin, Ph.D., Collaborating Editor

Published by Institute for Applied Neuroscience
31 College Place, Building B, Suite 210
Asheville, NC 28801

Printed in the United States of America

ISBN-13: 978-0692488898 (Institute for Applied Neuroscience)
ISBN-10: 0692488898

Dedication

This book is dedicated to my three lovable nephews,
Mathew, Andrew, and Luke, and my adorable niece, Nora.
May you always be healthy in mind, body, and spirit.

Acknowledgements

I would like to thank my friends and co-workers at The Institute for Applied Neuroscience: Ed, Pat, Illysa, Christie with a "C" and Kristy with a "K", Martha, and Steve. Thanks for being such a stellar team! Ed, an extra special thank you goes out to you. Obviously, this book would never have been written without you. You are the Jack Donaghy to my Liz Lemon.

I'd also like to thank my pals, Sarah Thomas, Raven Sinclaire, Jennifer T. Johnston, and Mindy Coleman, for providing encouragement and inspiration. Thank you to my writers' group friends: Sarah Henry Donnelly, Megan Lake, Kassandra Cummings, Melinda Bullen, and Amber Dollyhigh—long may we share our stories. To my Smoky Mountain Writers classmates—thank you for your feedback on earlier versions of this book. I am grateful to my family (The AmFam and, by extension, the Carters, Kantras, and Novaks). I love you all.

Thank you to my Pepperdine professor, David Elkins, for originally sharing my passion for non-pharmaceutical approaches to mental health.

I owe many thanks to my wonderful editor, Jennifer Hawthorne, and my meticulous proofreader, Doug McNair. I appreciate the myriad ways you guided me through this process and made this book better.

Last but not least, thanks to Dale Neal, my writing instructor, who always reminds me to get to the point.

Ten Facts You Should Know Before Making the Decision to Medicate Your Child

As a parent, it's undeniably frightening to realize that your child is having attention, behavioral, and/or academic problems that warrant professional intervention. It's understandable to want to find the quickest, most effective solution available to maximize your child's chances of social and academic success. In fact, this normal parental desire helps explain why millions of American children are currently taking psychotropic medications. Moreover, parents frequently receive pressure from educational or medical professionals to put their child on medication.

It is my hope, however, that this book will find its way into your hands *before* your first meeting with a prescriber. As parents, you have the tremendous responsibility of making the best decisions you can for your kids with the most accurate information you can gather. Before giving your child a pill to swallow or a medicated patch to wear, you need to know many important facts about their effects. But unfortunately, most prescribers won't tell you these things. Many of them may not even be aware of much of this information themselves.

In this e-book, I'll present ten critical facts you should know before medicating your child. The specific medications I'll be discussing are stimulants used to treat ADHD, antidepressants, and antipsychotics, the last of which are prescribed at an alarming rate for nonpsychotic people, even children. I'm including a great deal of science along with these facts, but I believe it's important to do so to authenticate the information I'm providing. I'll also describe some of the most effective noninvasive practices and therapies for children struggling from attention and behavioral problems. Knowledge of these methods is crucial for parents who want to understand *all* their options before turning to medication for their children.

However, if your child is already taking medication, **PLEASE DO NOT reduce, discontinue, or otherwise change the administration of your child's medication without consulting your prescriber first**. I will repeat this statement many times throughout this book because **there can be severe medical consequences if psychotropic drugs are suddenly stopped or abruptly reduced**. I recommend that you take this information to your prescriber and work with him or her to make informed, medically supervised decisions about whether or not to make any medication changes.

Just Who Am I to Be Giving Out This Information, Anyway?

That's a great question—I'm glad you asked. I'm a licensed psychologist with a doctoral degree in clinical psychology. Throughout my training, I've worked at a nonprofit child protective services agency, a VA hospital, three different juvenile detention centers, an adolescent outpatient substance abuse program, a university counseling center, and a state penitentiary. I've been working in private practice since 2004.

Since 2006, I've utilized a method of applied neuroscience called neurofeedback, or EEG brain-wave biofeedback. This specialized tool helps people improve their self-regulation skills. As a neurofeedback provider, I've learned a great deal about the EEG (electroencephalogram), which measures and records electrical activity in the brain, and how the human nervous system works. I've witnessed firsthand the negative side effects of psychotropic medications while also observing how noninvasive interventions such as effective parenting techniques, behavioral skills training, dietary changes, and neurofeedback can make lasting, positive changes in the lives and health of patients.

But most importantly, I care about children. I passionately believe that it is adults' and society's responsibility to protect them. The credo of my profession is "First, Do No Harm." I can no longer keep silent while well-meaning parents and medical professionals (as well as unscrupulous pharmaceutical companies) violate this edict in the name of mental health treatment. I don't want to be associated with a profession that does more harm than good. I'm not trying to sell you anything; I just want you to be truly informed before you consent to placing your child on psychotropic drugs.

The Importance of Diagnostic Agnosticism

Before jumping into the meat of this book, I need to provide some background information, explaining why neuroscience has shown certain accepted mental health approaches to be outdated. If science makes your eyes glaze over, you can skip this part. But if you can stick with me, I'll use the analogy of driving a car to share this information in a way that's easier to understand.

All of the providers in my clinic are avowed *diagnostic agnostics*. This term was promoted by my friend, mentor, and colleague, Dr. Ed Hamlin. I have adopted it ever since I first heard him say it. With his permission, I'm using it here.

Unlike medical diagnoses such as hypertension or diabetes, there are no tests that definitively determine a mental health diagnosis. Instead, we rely on symptom checklists. All of the diagnostic labels your child could be given—attention deficit hyperactivity disorder (ADHD), oppositional defiant disorder, Asperger's syndrome, reactive attachment disorder, bipolar disorder, and post-traumatic stress disorder (PTSD)—

are really just descriptions of clusters of subjective symptoms and observable behaviors.

As Dr. Hamlin says, getting one of these diagnoses is like going to your physician and receiving a diagnosis of "fever." That label, like the previously mentioned mental health diagnoses, merely describes the symptom—but the term *fever* does not adequately explain what is causing your body's temperature to rise. Similarly, a diagnosis of ADHD does not tell you what is causing your child's attention problems.

Luckily, advances in technology and brain-imaging techniques have granted us much greater ability to see what is physically occurring inside an individual's brain. Neurofeedback providers who study and train the EEG think in terms of "nervous-system arousal." *Arousal* roughly translates to a level of alertness and whether or not someone's focus is directed internally (when sleeping, daydreaming, or contemplating one's own private thoughts and feelings) or externally (when tuning into the direct experience of the current environment). When everything is working well, an individual's nervous system can effectively match its arousal level to the task at hand. In other words, the person can focus for as long as necessary to accomplish daily tasks, flexibly shift his or her attention from one task to another, let go and relax whenever appropriate, and enjoy a full night of restful sleep.

Unfortunately, many people have problems effectively regulating their nervous system arousal levels. For example, some individuals have difficulty getting their brain to focus long enough to complete necessary tasks, while others have a hard time shutting their mind off to go to sleep. Below, I'll describe five main types of arousal regulation problems that can interfere with people's functioning, as seen in EEG recordings.

First, the EEG can reflect patterns of nervous system *overarousal*—demonstrated by either a lack of idling brainwave activity; an excess of small, fast brain waves; or both. Patterns of overarousal are seen in people with "busy" brains, who often have difficulty relaxing or falling asleep and who can be prone to experiencing anxiety. When a brain doesn't idle sufficiently, its neurons miss out on opportunities to replenish themselves because they are constantly engaged. They're stuck in the "on" position. In other words, the brain is always in gear. This would be like attempting to drive a car all the way across the country but never turning the engine off long enough to refuel.

Overaroused people who have an excess of small, fast brain waves are like drivers who speed everywhere they go—they've got their foot slammed down on the accelerator. And some people have both issues involved in overarousal—they speed right past every gas station without stopping.

The second problematic EEG pattern is *underarousal*—an excess of bigger, slower brain waves, as seen in people with depression, low energy, frequent waking during the night, low motivation, and typical ADHD symptoms. A surplus of slow wave activity creates too much noise in the brain, which makes it difficult to get things done. This would be similar to driving your car up a mountain without realizing your emergency brake is on, a situation that would impede your speed. Another analogy would be a car engine that just isn't firing on all cylinders—the engine isn't activated enough to make it up the mountain.

The third problematic pattern of nervous system arousal is *dysregulated arousal*—which occurs when a person has both too much slow-wave *and* too much fast-wave activity. This would be like driving while pushing the gas and brake pedals at the same time. You can get to where you're going, but it's neither a very efficient use of your car's fuel or a very comfortable ride. Nevertheless, some people's nervous systems don't realize there's any other way to drive because they've always driven this way.

Another pattern is *unstable arousal*—rapidly switching between nervous system overarousal and underarousal—as seen in individuals with migraine headaches, seizures, emotional regulation problems, and high sensitivity to substances such as alcohol or caffeine. Do you remember the 2010 Toyota recall due to unintended acceleration? An unstable EEG pattern would be similar to your car suddenly—and unintendedly—either accelerating or braking, interfering with your ability to maintain a desired speed and increasing the likelihood of accidents.

And finally, there is *disordered arousal*—in which entire brain areas are overaroused while others are simultaneously underaroused. For example, the survival centers of a person's brain may be overactive while the calming, inhibitory centers may be underactive. Disordered arousal prevents brain networks from communicating and cooperating well with each other, and it is often seen in people with histories of childhood trauma and individuals described as being on the autism spectrum.

This EEG pattern could be likened to driving a car on which all four wheels are not turning at the same speed. As you can imagine, it would be extremely challenging to get where you wanted or needed to go in such a vehicle.

The five problematic patterns of nervous system arousal coincide with various symptoms. But sometimes a specific symptom, such as difficulty concentrating, can look the same outwardly yet have a very different underlying EEG pattern. For example, some people have trouble concentrating because the front parts of their brain have too much slow-wave activity and are not awake or alert enough to focus. Conversely, other people have trouble concentrating because their brain is so overly aroused that they quickly jump from thought to thought, fragmenting their attention and creating an internal distraction. Although both types of attention problems may result in similar outcomes—distractibility, difficulty concentrating in class, or poor grades—the primary cause of these problems is not the same. Consequently, children with different underlying EEG patterns are likely to respond to medication very differently as well.

To continue with our attention problem example, when most prescribers hear about distractibility and poor concentration, they immediately think of ADHD and stimulant medications. While the person with an underaroused brain may respond positively to treatment with stimulants (at least initially—this will be discussed further later), the person with an overly aroused brain may actually feel worse when given a stimulant. He might experience unpleasant and even serious side effects because stimulant medications increase the very type of brain waves he already has in excess.

As diagnostic agnostics, rather than getting caught up in finding the best descriptive diagnostic label, we investigate what is physically occurring in someone's brain that could be contributing to his or her problems. We do this so that we can then identify the most effective intervention methods for the patient's condition. Unfortunately, the majority of prescribers are unaware that simple EEG measurements exist to aid this process.

Besides taking kids' EEG patterns into account, there are other equally important reasons for diagnostic agnosticism. Sometimes, a child's brain waves might be exactly the way we would expect them to be for her age, but she may be living in a chaotic, abusive, or stressful environment. Or he might have experienced the loss of a loved one or undergone a traumatic medical procedure. Perhaps she is experiencing social pressures or problems, such as bullying. If a child is worried about getting beaten up on the playground or his parents divorcing, his attention to schoolwork is likely to suffer. In addition, sometimes children have specific food or environmental allergies that affect their emotional and cognitive functioning. Or there may be some underlying metabolic issues or lingering effects from a complicated birth. These are just a few of the variables that can affect children's behaviors.

Because children's brains are still in the process of developing; individual children develop at different rates; and myriad emotional, situational, and environmental factors exist that can affect their behaviors make the notion of diagnostic agnosticism especially important when conceptualizing and addressing children's problems.

Now that we've acknowledged the importance of considering all the possible variables that could be causing, perpetuating, or exacerbating your child's difficulties, we can proceed with the 10 facts all parents should know before making the decision to medicate their children. Following that section, I'll describe the most effective noninvasive methods and techniques to help your child without resorting to medication as a first step.

The Ten Facts

#1 There are two attention networks in the brain: one in the front of the head and one in the back. If your child's problem is in the back of the brain, stimulant medications can only provide a temporary "override" of the faulty posterior network. Stimulants won't correct what's causing the underlying issue. And even if your child's problem is in the front of the brain, relying on medications will actually weaken the frontal lobe rather than strengthening it.

To discuss this point, we must first briefly review a few neuroanatomy notes. In the course of human maturation, the back of the brain develops first while the frontal lobe is the last part of the brain to wire up. The frontal lobe is considered to be the "executive functioning center" because it's in charge of good judgment, impulse control, motivation, learning from experience, and foreseeing consequences, as well as planning and initiating behaviors. The frontal lobe doesn't finish developing until somewhere around age 25. (This is why teenagers give their parents so many sleepless nights—adolescents' brains are not mature enough to consistently make good decisions.)

The frontal lobe is also the seat of our voluntary attention network: it allows us to choose where we want to focus our awareness. The back of the brain is evolutionarily older, develops first, and is more concerned with survival. It houses our involuntary, or reflexive, attention network. For example, even if you're completely engrossed in reading a best-selling novel, if you hear an unexpected loud noise behind you, you'll reflexively look to see what caused that noise in order to ensure your safety is not at risk. The two attention networks should work together to help a person focus on the most important details of his or her current experience.

To this end, the human brain evolved to have an ordered flow of information. All the sensory information coming from inside and outside the body goes to the back of the brain first, where it's integrated into a perception; then it's sent to the middle of the brain for processing and comparison with previous memories; and then it goes to the front, where the person decides what, if anything, to do in response to this integrated information. In other words, there is supposed to be a smooth, continuous informational flow as follows: input (back of the brain), processing (middle of the brain), output or behavior (front of the brain). The person's output, or behavior interfacing with the environment, then becomes part of the next informational input, and the cycle continues.

Because we can't possibly absorb and consciously process every single detail of our existence, the back of the brain is supposed to automatically filter out information that is extraneous or irrelevant to the task at hand. But sometimes this filter, which really functions more like a gate, is faulty. The gate might be thrown wide open, letting in a flood of information, so that the middle and front of the brain become overwhelmed. Or the gate might be tightly shut, thereby denying the brain important details. Or in the case of hypervigilance, the back of the brain might be so overly concerned with identifying any possible threats to survival that it continuously hijacks the individual's awareness. After all, the brain's number-one job is to keep itself alive, so environmental stimuli that seem like potential threats are always going to take precedence over academic lessons.

Whatever your child's attentional issues might be, stimulant medications only "work" because they temporarily increase the frontal lobe's ability to maintain its focus on repetitive tasks. If your child's problem is in the posterior input areas, stimulant medications can artificially boost the front of the brain's ability to override distractions caused by the faulty filter in the back of the head. In other words, the medications temporarily enable the frontal lobe to press on the gas pedal more strongly. However, as soon as the medicine is no longer in your child's system, the original problem returns.

Even if the back of your child's brain is working just fine and the problem lies in the front, relying on stimulant medications actually weakens the frontal lobe because the brain becomes dependent upon this outside chemical to do its job. The brain doesn't learn how to use its own resources effectively, so again, once the medication has worn off, the problem is still there.

The good news is that there are many ways to naturally strengthen your child's frontal lobe. Delaying gratification, following daily routines and schedules, engaging in regular physical exercise, getting adequate sleep and hydration, eating healthy foods (while avoiding certain processed foods), and playing strategic games that require planning (such as checkers) all help strengthen the frontal lobe (more on this later).

In fact, parents themselves are supposed to act as mature, external frontal lobes for their children until their children's brains have had enough time to develop. Allowing children to make age-appropriate decisions when possible and practical also helps their frontal lobe learn from experience in safe ways. For more information, please see the suggested reading list for recommended parenting books.

#2 If ADHD medications are effective at all, they're only effective in the short term.

The National Institute for Mental Health's Multimodal Treatment Study of Children with Attention Deficit Hyperactivity Disorder (MTA) recently revealed this important fact. The MTA study followed 579 elementary school children (ages 7 to 9) who had been diagnosed with ADHD. The children were randomly assigned to one of four treatment groups: (1) medication only, (2) behavioral treatment only, (3) a combination of medication and behavioral treatment, and (4) supportive services in communities and schools. The children's progress was closely monitored for 14 months. After that time period, the participating families were allowed to choose which treatment method they wanted to use for their children. Follow-up assessments were conducted a year after the original 14-month study had concluded, then 2 years later, and again 8 years later (MTA Cooperative Group, 1999).

The study's preliminary findings suggested that treatment options 1 (medication only) and 3 (a combination of behavioral treatment and medication) were both better at reducing ADHD symptoms than options 2 (behavioral treatment only) and 4 (supportive services only). However, the study showed that the initial advantages of medication (whether used alone or in combination with other interventions) gradually diminished over time (MTA Cooperative Group, 1999).

According to follow-up assessments conducted 2 years later, continued treatment with medication was no longer associated with better outcomes in comparison to behavioral treatment only or supportive services (MTA Cooperative Group, 2007). In fact, later follow-ups actually showed that children who had taken stimulant medications were *worse* off than children who had never taken stimulants in terms of their physical health, and were no better off in terms of their academic or social success (Labbe, 2009; Molina et al., 2007; Whitaker, 2010).

One of the coauthors of the MTA study, William E. Pelham, MD, stated that the study's findings added to a large body of literature failing to find "any evidence of beneficial effects of stimulant medications on ADHD children's long-term outcomes" (Stump, 2009, pp. 8–9). In a 2009 *Neurology Now* article, Dr. Pelham also stated, "Parents should not expect long-term benefits from medication. And if treatment begins with medication, it undermines the probability of parents and schools engaging in appropriate non-drug treatments" (Stump, 2009, pp. 8–9). In fact, Pelham conducted another study that showed that when parents were instructed to implement behavioral interventions first, before ever being given a prescription for their child, 95% of them followed through with the behavioral recommendations. On the other hand, when parents were given a medication prescription first and *then* told to put their child in behavioral intervention programs, 75% failed to do so (Vedantam, 2009). Dr. Pelham concluded, "Parents should insist that doctors hook them up with appropriate providers of evidence-based psychosocial treatments and that their insurance pay for those treatments. I'm concerned that medication is being increasingly used as the first and sole intervention for ADHD, and that parents are being told that medication will help in the long run, when the evidence is very clear that it will not" (Stump, 2009, pp. 8–9).

#3 Stimulant medications have been shown to stunt children's growth.

The previously mentioned MTA study found an additional significant difference between the children who took medication to treat their ADHD symptoms and those who did not: The kids who remained on the medicine were smaller in terms of height and weight than were their unmedicated counterparts (Vedantam, 2009). Specifically, the medicated children were approximately one inch shorter and six pounds lighter. Other studies have also demonstrated that stimulant medications inhibit the production of growth hormone, which is involved in building muscle and bone (Glasser, 2005). Apparently, the overproduction of dopamine created by stimulant medications suppresses the production of this important hormone in the pituitary gland. Although this disruption may sometimes be reversible once a child stops taking stimulants, the exact time frame before the effects become permanent is unknown (Glasser, 2005).

Besides suppressing growth, other reported adverse effects of stimulant medications include appetite loss, difficulty sleeping, lethargy, jaw clenching, facial and vocal tics, abdominal pain, headaches, weight loss, liver problems, hypertension, sudden cardiac death, depression, mood swings, apathy, crying spells, irritability, anxiety, hostility, obsessive-compulsive thoughts and behaviors, mania, paranoia, and psychosis (Whitaker, 2010; Glasser, 2005).

Please remember, if you or your children are currently taking any psychotropic medications, do not make any changes in the amount or frequency of your dosage until you speak with your prescriber! Suddenly stopping or abruptly reducing medications can have negative physical and mental health consequences. Talk to your prescriber about any concerns you may have.

#4 Long-term use of stimulant medications may leave your child vulnerable to depression.

Stimulant medications are amphetamines, meaning they belong to the same class of drugs as does cocaine. All amphetamines affect dopaminergic reward pathways in the brain, which are involved in making us feel good and creating our sense of joy. It's well established that chronic cocaine use can permanently damage these pathways. Animal studies suggest that repeated exposure to methylphenidate—such as Ritalin, a common medication used to treat ADHD—might do the same.

Researchers at Texas Southwestern Medical Center in Dallas exposed young (what would be considered "preadolescent") rats to Ritalin for 15 days (Bolaños, Barrot, Berton, Wallace-Black, & Nestler, 2003). The animals turned into anxious creatures who displayed signs of depression as adults. They were less physically active, less responsive to natural rewards such as sugar, less likely to engage with or explore new environments, and less interested in sexual activity. Moreover, the rats treated with methylphenidate were "significantly more sensitive to stressful situations, showed increased anxiety-like behaviors, and had enhanced plasma levels of corticosterone (a stress hormone)" (Bolaños, Barrot, Berton, Wallace-Black, & Nestler, 2003). The authors stated that exposing rats to Ritalin while their brains were still developing resulted in "aberrant behavioral adaptations during adulthood" (Bolaños, Barrot, Berton, Wallace-Black, & Nestler, 2003).

Once again, if you or your kids are currently taking any psychotropic medications, do not reduce, discontinue, or make any other medication changes without first consulting your prescriber! Suddenly stopping or abruptly reducing medications can have negative consequences.

#5 Diet can impact your child's symptoms of ADHD and/or autism.

There is a rapidly expanding body of literature suggesting that certain foods exacerbate symptoms of ADHD and autism. By eliminating or reducing the number of sugary junk foods and highly processed foods with dyes, artificial colors, and preservatives, as well as gluten (a protein in wheat) and dairy products (butter, milk, and cheese) that they feed their children, many parents have seen significant improvements in their children's behaviors. In fact, a recent comprehensive review of nutritional studies revealed that foods with artificial colors were particularly culpable in exacerbating ADHD symptoms (Sonuga-Barke et al., 2013). This meta-analysis also provided evidence that giving kids Omega 3 and 6 fatty-acid supplements can decrease symptoms of ADHD. I also know of a psychiatrist specializing in ADHD who recommends that parents eliminate gluten and dairy from their children's diet for six months. If, after that amount of time, the child is still exhibiting symptoms of ADHD, then and only then does he consider prescribing medication. According to him, at least half of the children respond so well to dietary changes that they do not require further intervention.

I understand that altering your child's diet may seem impossible at first, but if you just focus on making small changes by choosing healthy foods whenever possible, it can make a difference. I have personal experience with this issue. In 2010, I had to eliminate gluten and dairy from my own diet, and although it seemed overwhelming initially, it became manageable very quickly. I realize that kids can present special challenges in this regard, but as previously mentioned, if you commit to following dietary guidelines as best you can, you are likely to see some benefits. As more and more people jump on the gluten- and dairy-free bandwagon, it is becoming much easier to find tasty and convenient gluten-free and dairy-free foods. Please see the suggested reading list for dietary resources.

#6 If your child is considered to be on the autism spectrum, you need to know that to date, no medication has been found to correct autism's symptoms. Most of the time, medications prescribed for autism spectrum disorders merely sedate the child to make him or her less disruptive.

Here again, I need to explain this statement from what I know about the EEG. At my clinic, we've seen the "brain maps" of many children with an autism spectrum diagnosis. What we've seen, and what the literature shows, is that these children frequently have a disordered pattern of nervous system arousal that results in important brain networks not communicating well with one another. This is known as a "connectivity" problem. Sometimes these brain networks are operating at different speeds. Much as with relay race teammates who can't adequately match their running pace and end up dropping the baton, important information gets lost in these kids' brains.

At this time, we don't have any medications that correct connectivity problems in the brain. That's because the medications available today can't limit or localize their effects to specific networks. Instead, medications have general, global effects on brain areas or the entire nervous system. Since medicines are not sophisticated enough to correct the underlying connectivity problem, they just treat certain symptoms. Unfortunately, this symptom management usually comes at the cost of unwanted side effects. Most often, prescribers tend to give sedating medications (such as antipsychotics) to kids described as being on the autism spectrum so that their behaviors will be more compliant and less disruptive. While this might make such children more manageable in the classroom, it does not help them learn to think critically, develop social skills, or engage with their peers. In fact, kids are more likely to withdraw and keep to themselves when under the influence of sedating medications.

#7 Your child's brain is still in the process of developing and "wiring itself up." More often than not, medications interfere with this process by adding greater abnormalities to the EEG instead of correcting any existing abnormalities.

We send all of our quantitative EEG recordings to university medical center neurologists for a medical review before we do anything else with the information. These experts specialize in examining EEGs for any abnormal activity that would indicate a medical problem, such as seizures or a possible brain tumor. If the neurologist doesn't realize that a client had medications in her system at the time we took the recording, they frequently tell us the EEG is medically abnormal due to an excess of both fast and slow brain-wave activity. The official term they use is *encephalopathic*. Once the neurologists realize the person was taking medications at the time of the EEG, however, they change their description of the EEG from "medically abnormal" to "an excess of fast and slow brain-wave activity consistent with medication effects."

Introducing these chemically induced abnormalities into a brain that is still developing throws everything off. We're not even completely sure how far-reaching those effects will be because they are not yet known. We have to wait for a generation of medicated children to grow up before we'll really have any idea. Likewise, we've only recently been able to measure the long-term effects psychotropic medications have had on adults who've been taking them continuously for decades. The results are sobering. Chronic use of antianxiety medications (benzodiazepines), antidepressants (SSRIs), and antipsychotics (neuroleptics) are all associated with *worse* outcomes (Whitaker, 2010). Studies have shown that people who remain on medications over the long term are more likely to apply for disability for mental health reasons (Whitaker, 2010). These people frequently gain a significant amount of weight, which puts them at greater risk for a multitude of physical issues, including high blood pressure, diabetes, and heart disease. Long-term use of antipsychotic drugs can cause permanent motor tics and/or movement disorders. Moreover, antidepressant and antipsychotic medications have been associated with forgetfulness, memory loss, and even higher rates of earlier-onset dementia (Jackson, 2009). Similarly, benzodiazepines (Xanax, Klonopin, Valium, Ativan) have been associated with a 50% increase in the risk of dementia (Billoti de Gage et al., 2012).

These reported outcomes for adults are disturbing, so it's deeply troubling to think about the potential damage that could occur if kids start taking these substances earlier in life and stay on them even longer. **Nevertheless, if you or your children are currently taking any psychotropic medications, do not make any changes in the amount or frequency of your dosage until you speak with your prescriber first! Suddenly stopping or abruptly reducing medications is not a good idea (especially with benzodiazepines) unless you are medically advised to do so and are medically supervised during the process.**

#8 Antidepressant medications increase the risk of suicide in children and young adults.

You may recall news stories about parents suing pharmaceutical companies because their children demonstrated increased suicidality (meaning suicidal thoughts and behaviors) after starting SSRI medications. (SSRI stands for selective serotonin reuptake inhibitors; SSRIs include Prozac, Paxil, Luvox, Lexapro, Celexa, and Zoloft, among others). These lawsuits spurred the FDA to hold a special hearing in 2004 to investigate this potential increased risk (FDA, 2009). Consequently, the FDA determined that initiating SSRI medication actually doubled the risk of suicidality in adolescents and young adults (FDA, 2005). As a result, pharmaceutical companies are now legally required to list increased risk of suicide in children and young adults as a potential side effect of SSRI medications. But that doesn't mean that consumers are told this information before they're given a prescription. In my experience, some parents have only heard about this risk because they researched the medication themselves or actually took the time to read the drug facts provided by the pharmacy filling their child's prescription. I'm concerned that many prescribers fail to discuss the increased risk of suicide when recommending SSRI medications for children and young adults.

The FDA also recommends that children and adolescents have weekly face-to-face meetings with their prescriber for the first few months after beginning treatment with an SSRI medication, as well as whenever there is a change in dosage, whether it be an increase or decrease (FDA, 2005). In addition, the FDA guidelines stress the importance of informing parents of the need to closely monitor their kids for any signs of agitation, irritability, unusual changes in behavior, psychomotor restlessness (known as *akathisia*), hypomania, and mania, as well as suicidal thoughts and behaviors (Whitaker, 2010). Again, I'm concerned that many prescribers fail to follow these guidelines when prescribing antidepressant medications to juveniles.

What's equally alarming is that the risks of prescribing antidepressant medications to children and adolescents seem to outweigh any benefits. Antidepressants have not demonstrated very high success rates with minors (FDA, 2005). Prozac is the only antidepressant that the FDA has determined to have some (albeit limited) benefit for use in treating pediatric depression, so at the time of this writing, it's the only antidepressant that is FDA approved for kids (FDA, 2005). If a prescriber is using any medication other than Prozac to treat your child's depression, you should have been informed that the drug is being used "off-label," which means it is being used in an unapproved way. Prozac, Zoloft, Luvox, and Anafranil are SSRI medications that are FDA approved to treat obsessive-compulsive disorder in children and adolescents (APA, 1994), but Prozac is the only medication approved for treating pediatric depression.

Remember, if you or your children are currently taking any psychotropic medications, do not reduce, discontinue, or otherwise make any medication changes until you first consult your prescriber! Suddenly stopping or radically reducing medications—especially antidepressant medications—can have negative consequences.

#9 The diagnosis of bipolar disorder never used to be given to children—only to adults. Only recently has this changed, and the psychiatrist who popularized the notion of "pediatric bipolar disorder" was caught taking over a million dollars from pharmaceutical companies. Moreover, a child's "bipolar" symptoms can actually be caused by previous use of stimulant and/or antidepressant medications.

Bipolar disorder (formerly called manic-depressive illness) used to be thought of as a relatively rare condition (affecting about 1 in 10,000 people) that was most likely to show up when someone was in his or her twenties (Whitaker, 2010). The defining feature of bipolar disorder is the experience of at least one manic episode, which is supposed to last for a period of seven days and involve either a euphoric, expansive, or irritable mood with at least three of the following symptoms (or four if the person's mood is only irritable): heightened self-esteem/grandiosity, decreased need for sleep, increased talkativeness with rapid and pressured speech, flight of ideas, distractibility, increased psychomotor or goal-directed activity, and poor judgment. These symptoms are supposed to be severe enough to do one of the following: cause psychotic symptoms; require hospitalization to protect the person's safety; or significantly impair the person's functioning in work, social, or personal situations (Whitaker, 2010).

Conventional wisdom held that children, especially children under the age of 13, did not exhibit manic symptoms. In fact, it was such a rare occurrence that physicians regularly emphasized the importance of refraining from giving kids a manic-depressive or bipolar diagnosis. But then this thinking gradually started changing, and in the 1990s, there was a veritable explosion in the number of reported cases of "juvenile bipolar disorder" (Whitaker, 2010). What could possibly account for this dramatic change? What most people don't realize is that a very high percentage of "bipolar" children discussed in the scientific literature were treated with some type of medication (most often stimulant or antidepressant medications) before they ever demonstrated any manic symptoms. And rather than making the logical connection that the drugs may have *caused* the manic symptoms and behaviors, several psychiatrists and drug companies purported the belief that the drugs merely "unmasked" the child's underlying propensity for bipolar illness, which supposedly already existed.

But doesn't it seem strange that the diagnosis of bipolar disorder in children and adolescents suddenly and dramatically increased 40-fold from 1995 to 2003 (Harris & Carey, 2008)? 25 out of every 10,000 kids were diagnosed with pediatric bipolar disorder in 1995. This number jumped to 1,003 out of every 10,000 children in 2003 (Moreno, et al., 2007). This huge increase in the number of kids diagnosed with bipolar disorder—a condition that never used to be considered a childhood illness—had a direct relationship with the increase in prescriptions of stimulant and antidepressant medications given to children. Furthermore, one of the psychiatrists responsible for loosening the criteria necessary for the diagnosis of juvenile bipolar disorder was Harvard psychiatrist Joseph Biederman. In 2008, Dr. Biederman was involved in a well-publicized scandal when *The New York Times* revealed he had taken $1.6 million in consulting fees from pharmaceutical companies (Powers, 2008). Dr. Biederman failed to report the funds he had taken, and in the professional papers he wrote on this topic, he failed to acknowledge that his taking of such funds created a conflict of interest.

#10 Abilify, Seroquel, Geodon, Risperdal, and their generic versions are all antipsychotic medications that have potentially permanent, dangerous side effects.

If you are an American who watches network television, chances are pretty good that you've seen commercials urging you to ask your doctor if Abilify would be an appropriate medication for you. In the ads, you're likely to see scenes of happy people walking on the beach or otherwise enjoying themselves. What you're not told is that Abilify is a powerful antipsychotic medication.

People who have never experienced any psychotic symptoms really have no business taking antipsychotic medications. These drugs are known as neuroleptics, and they have a long list of potentially adverse effects, some of which can be permanent (Powers, 2008). The most common negative side effects are movement disorders, which affect the involuntary motor system and can result in the following conditions (Powers, 2008):

- *Tardive dyskinesia*, which is the development of repetitive, tic-like movements that primarily occur in the facial muscles (such as tongue thrusting and lip smacking) but can also occur in the limbs, fingers, and toes
- *Dystonia*, which is the chronic spasming of certain muscles such as the neck, which can be life threatening if left untreated
- *Akathisia*, which is psychomotor restlessness that can

feel very uncomfortable and appear as agitation

- *Pseudo-Parkinsonism*, which is drug-induced symptoms of Parkinson's disease, including slow movements, shuffling gait, stiffness of the limbs and neck, and muscle rigidity

Older neuroleptic medications, known as "first-generation antipsychotics," are most likely to cause these movement disorders; however, the newer second- and third-generation antipsychotic medications can also cause them (Muench & Hamer, 2010). It just may take longer for the adverse effects to appear. But if your child starts taking the medication at four years of age and there's no plan in place to take him or her off the medications, he or she has a lifetime to develop these symptoms. No prescriber can predict when someone might develop the symptoms, and to date, there is no known prevention or cure other than reducing the dose, discontinuing the medicine, or switching to a different medication that has a lower risk of these side effects. Sometimes movement disorders are reversible once they appear, but unfortunately, sometimes they are not (Powers, 2008).

Other serious side effects of neuroleptic medications include weight gain and metabolic changes that increase your child's risk of diabetes. Similarly, all antipsychotic medications can produce additional medical complications, including glucose and lipid intolerance, cardiac conduction problems, increased risk of seizure (Muench & Hamer, 2010), and changes in the way the body metabolizes other medications (Powers, 2008).

Up until 2007, no antipsychotic medications were approved by the FDA to be used by children or adolescents (Avigan, Brinker, & Diak, 2009). In 2009, however, multiple second-generation neuroleptics were approved for juveniles with the specific diagnoses of schizophrenia, Bipolar I disorder, or irritability associated with autism (Reinberg, 2009). During the drug approval process, many medical professionals expressed grave concerns about the potential side effects of these medications (Harris, 2008). Several experts emphasized the need for caution when using neuroleptics with a pediatric population.

Nevertheless, recent studies have shown a disturbing increase in the number of antipsychotic medicines prescribed for children, regardless of their diagnoses. A study conducted by the Children's Hospital of Philadelphia in 2012 found a 62% increase over the past decade in the number of antipsychotic medications given to children, ages 3 to 18, enrolled in Medicaid (Matone et al., 2012). Although the diagnoses of schizophrenia, bipolar disorder, and autism were most likely to result in the prescription of antipsychotics, young people with these disorders did not make up the majority of antipsychotic users. Of the participants included in this study, kids with ADHD accounted for 50% of antipsychotic use in the year 2007. According to the authors, one in seven antipsychotic users was a child with ADHD as his or her only diagnosis. But the largest group of children taking antipsychotic medications by far consisted of kids who had been given three or more co-occurring mental health diagnoses (Matone et al., 2012). A study published in 2005 examining prescribing trends for children enrolled in three state Medicaid programs demonstrated strikingly similar results (Patel et al., 2005). From 1996 to 2001, total antipsychotic use increased significantly across all the regions included in the study. In the Midwest, antipsychotic prescriptions increased from 4.7 to 14.3 per 1,000 children; in the South, they increased from 6.3 to 15.5; and in the West, they increased from 4.5 to 6.9 (Patel et al., 2005). It's worth noting that the time period involved in this study included years in which no antipsychotic medications were even FDA approved for pediatric use.

At this point, you might find yourself thinking, "OK, so if drugs are not the answer, then what is?" We will address this excellent question in the next section.

Nonmedicinal, Noninvasive Approaches to Helping Children

Driving analogies work well to illustrate patterns of nervous system arousal because each of us is the operator of his or her own body. Much as our automobiles need regular maintenance to keep them in working order, our nervous systems also depend on regular maintenance to keep them functioning. For humans, this means maintaining a regular sleep/wake cycle, eating a healthy diet, getting adequate exercise, limiting screen time (TV, computer/tablet, videogames, and smartphones), participating in positive social interactions, and practicing effective stress management skills. Structuring this regular maintenance for children is a tremendous parenting responsibility because no matter whether your child takes medicine or not, if one of these key components is missing, the functioning of his or her nervous system will be suboptimal.

Most animals and humans fare better with predictable routines. Of course, this does not mean that there is no room for spontaneity or adventure; life would be unbearably boring without these two ingredients. Nevertheless, keeping to healthy routines ensures that important self-care activities are completed, and this ultimately frees up more time and energy for other experiences. If you don't already have a regular daily routine for your family, I recommend you create one. No matter what your child's problems might be, providing predictable structure can only help him or her. The essential components of a healthy routine are described in more detail below.

Regular Sleep/Wake Cycle

When you maintain a regular sleep/wake cycle for your child, it means that he or she goes to bed at roughly the same time every night and gets up at roughly the same time every morning. Experts say that wake-up times and bedtimes should not vary by more than a half hour from day to day. Sticking to a regular sleep schedule helps everyone's brain know when it's time to be alert and awake and when it's time to replenish itself through sleep. Children's and adolescents' brains typically need more sleep than do those of adults. This is because they are still developing and are thus working hard to construct important brain networks and consolidate learning.

Research shows that modern-day children are getting 60 to 75 fewer minutes of sleep every night than did children 100 years ago (Matricciani, Olds, & Petkov, 2012). Since sleep is cyclical in nature, repeatedly moving from lighter stages to deeper ones, and since the most restorative elements of sleep occur in the deeper stages, getting fewer hours of sleep means experiencing at least one less cycle of the deepest sleep stages per night.

Interestingly, the trend of children sleeping less is positively correlated with higher rates of ADHD symptoms (Astill, Van der Heijden, Van Ijzendoorn, & Van Someren, 2012). Sleep deprivation can mimic a host of ills, such as attention problems, mood disorders (including irritability and mood swings), and even psychotic symptoms. I've known three college students who wound up in mental hospitals simply because they were exhausted from pulling too many all-nighters. Their chronically sleep-deprived brains began exhibiting symptoms of severe mental illness. But as soon as their sleep was restored, those symptoms disappeared.

It's also important to note that as young children become overly tired, they are likely to exhibit symptoms of hyperactivity rather than fatigue. You may have noticed your sons and/or daughters beginning to "bounce off the walls" if they stay up past their regular bedtimes. This is because the part of their brain that applies the brakes to their nervous system has become exhausted and is no longer performing its job well. Those braking mechanisms have to restore themselves through sleep.

Good Nutrition

Your brain derives the nutrients it needs to create neurotransmitters (chemical messengers) from the foods that you eat. So to state it bluntly, garbage in = garbage out. Sugar, artificial dyes, and preservatives, as well as—for some kids—gluten and dairy products, have been implicated in worsening children's attention and behavioral problems (Stevens, Kuczek, Burgess, Hurt, & Arnold, 2011). Providing whole, natural foods whenever possible reduces your child's exposure to these potentially harmful ingredients.

At my clinic, we've seen several children whose behavior problems improved significantly simply in response to dietary changes. One parent reported that his daughter, who was under three years old at the time, had been having multiple emotional "meltdowns" every single day. Her behavior was so disruptive that it interfered with her parents' accomplishing important daily tasks because they had to spend so much time managing her tantrums. She was also exhibiting chronic digestive issues in the form of diarrhea and loose stools. Once gluten was removed from her diet, however, her digestion problems cleared up and her meltdowns diminished from multiple times a day to once or twice a month.

Limited Screen Time

Research shows that parents should limit their children's nonproductive screen time to 10 hours a week. *Nonproductive* means not related to homework or other academic pursuits. According to one study, every hour of screen time above 10 per week negatively impacted children's academic performance (Williams, Haertel, Haertel, & Walberg, 1982). Increased screen time may also be one reason children are sleeping less these days. Prolonged exposure to blue light emitted from LED screens, especially late in the day, can disrupt people's natural circadian rhythms and significantly delay sleep onset (Arns, M., Feddema, I., & Kenemans, J. L., 2014). Sleep experts recommend that people of all ages refrain from exposing themselves to light from LED screens for at least one hour before bedtime.

Spending too much time on electronic devices also interferes with children's going outside to play and interact with their peers. An interesting study recently examined the relationship between sun exposure and rates of ADHD diagnoses (Arns, Van der Heijden, Arnold, & Kenemans, 2013). Researchers found that children who live in areas with greater sun exposure have lower rates of ADHD, while those who live in less sunny areas have higher rates of ADHD. Less time spent playing outside is also associated with increased rates of childhood obesity (Han, Lawlor, & Kimm, 2010), a widely acknowledged epidemic in America.

Ample, Consistent Exercise

Our brains and bodies evolved to be in motion. The very first nervous system consisted of sensory input and motor (movement) output. Primitive organisms perceived information from their environments and began to move toward food and energy sources and away from predators and other threats. From those humble origins arose the complex human bodies we inhabit today.

It's no wonder we feel better when we're moving: exercise releases endorphins, our bodies' natural feel-good chemicals. It also increases the flow of oxygen to the brain, keeps blood vessels supple, and ensures that newly born brain cells survive long enough to be recruited into the networks where they are needed the most. Children with symptoms of ADHD need at least 30 minutes of moderate to intense physical activity per day to enhance their brain functioning (Amen, 2013; Halperin & Healey, 2011). In fact, children who have difficulty focusing on homework often do better if they are given an opportunity to run around the yard or engage in some other form of movement to burn off energy first. Frequent, short breaks allowing physical activity can also help. Similarly, schools that specialize in educating children on the autism spectrum often find creative ways of incorporating self-soothing movements such as rocking, spinning, or jumping at appropriate times during the school day.

Positive Social Interactions

An ever-increasing body of evidence emphasizes the importance of positive social relationships in the maintenance of mental health and emotional well-being (Horstman, 2012). Parents can help their kids with this area of life by making time each day to interact with their children, including reading aloud to them, helping them with homework, conversing with them (which involves genuinely listening to them), and playing games. This may sound like a no-brainer, but since most American parents have to work outside the home, they are often left with precious little time for family interaction. Moreover, parents are often distracted by their own life stressors and electronic devices. It's not uncommon to see an entire family sitting silently in a room together with each person focused on his or her own electronic device. (I've witnessed this in my own family.) Lack of social interaction prevents kids from learning important interpersonal skills as well as experiencing the comforting stress relief that human connection can bring.

Children crave attention from their parents, and for most kids, negative attention is better than no attention at all. Setting aside time to give your child your undivided attention can do a great deal to ward off acting-out behaviors. Moreover, kids develop their sense of identity by how they see themselves reflected through interactions with the significant adults in their lives. A strong sense of identity helps kids successfully resist peer pressure to engage in dangerous and unhealthy behaviors.

Consider designating time for at least one regularly scheduled family activity each week. Family members can take turns selecting the activity for the week (of course, it must be parentally approved and appropriate for all ages involved). Not only does this preserve time for interaction and connection, but it also conveys respect for each family member's voice, preferences, and interests.

Effective Stress Management Skills

Stress management skills help children effectively cope with feelings of anxiety, anger, disappointment, and frustration. The very best way parents can help their kids learn these skills is by example. The better you are at managing such unpleasant emotions yourself, the better your children will be at it. As is true of many areas of parenting, when it comes to stress management, actions definitely speak louder than words. Diaphragmatic "belly" breathing, mindfulness strategies, guided relaxation exercises, drawing, and journaling are examples of healthy stress-management skills parents and children can use together. The children's book *Mindful Monkey, Happy Panda* by Lauren Alderfer describes mindfulness in a way kids can understand. *The Whole-Brain Child: 12 Revolutionary Strategies to Nurture Your Child's Developing Mind, Survive Everyday Parenting Struggles, and Help Your Family Thrive* by Daniel J.

Siegel, MD, and Tina Payne Bryson, PhD; and *The Mindful Child: How to Help Your Kid Manage Stress and Become Happier, Kinder, and More Compassionate* by Susan Kaiser Greenland are two other valuable resources for learning stress management skills.

Authoritative Parenting Style and Positive Discipline

Some parents are authoritarian (undisputed dictators). Some are overly permissive; in their households anything goes and the kids, rather than the adults, are in control. An authoritative approach is somewhere in the middle and yields the best results (Bornstein & Bornstein, 2007). Authoritative parents are kind but firm. Although they're respectful in their communications with their children, they also have clear rules and expectations, which they appropriately enforce. Another distinguishing characteristic of this parenting style is allowing children to make choices that are suitable to the children's age, such as what shirt to wear or what vegetable to have for dinner.

I realize that an authoritative parenting style is much easier to describe than to implement. Parenting is arguably life's most challenging job. Although children are wonderfully curious and often joyful and creative, they can also be demanding, exhausting, and difficult. No one is born knowing how to be an effective parent. Consequently, it pays to seek help from experts in child development. Parenting books I recommend are *Transforming the Difficult Child: The Nurtured Heart Approach* by Howard Glasser, MA, and Jennifer Easley, MA; *Parenting with Love and Logic: Teaching Children Responsibility* by Foster Cline, MD, and Jim Fay; and *Yes, Your Teen is Crazy: Loving Your Kid Without Losing Your Mind* by Michael J. Bradley, EdD.

Neurofeedback

If you've implemented all these important lifestyle changes and your child is still experiencing difficulties, another non-medicinal approach is worth considering. Neurofeedback, also known as EEG biofeedback, can help resolve problems with nervous system arousal. It's like driving school for nervous systems. Underaroused brains can learn to disengage the emergency brake; overaroused brains can take their feet off the gas pedal, shift into a lower gear, and idle better; unstably aroused brains can improve their ability to maintain a constant speed; dysregulated brains can learn to apply the gas and brake separately instead of simultaneously; and disordered brains can improve their connectivity.

Neurofeedback is a noninvasive technique that measures your child's brain-wave activity using sensors on the scalp or forehead. Once your child's EEG activity is "read" by the computer, it holds up a mirror to your child's brain so your child's brain can adjust its performance. It's like replacing a faulty car speedometer with a more effective one, helping the driver obtain and maintain the desired speed.

During a neurofeedback session, the computer provides visual and auditory feedback to inform your child when he or she is in the optimal range of brain-wave activity. By repeatedly practicing operating at an appropriate speed, your child can reset his or her nervous system. When human nervous systems experience a more energy-efficient method of functioning often enough, they will eventually adopt it, especially if it both feels and works better.

Neurofeedback may sound like science fiction, but it has actually been around since the 1960s. Over 1,000 studies have been conducted on this form of self-regulation training, and additional studies are currently underway. Empirical evidence supports its use with ADHD, epilepsy, anxiety, addictive disorders, depression, traumatic brain injuries, autistic spectrum disorders, learning disabilities, and migraine headaches.

Two stringent meta-analyses (extensive reviews of existing studies) of neurofeedback— one conducted in 2005 and the other conducted in 2009—are noteworthy. The 2005 meta-analysis concluded that EEG biofeedback (neurofeedback) meets criteria for "clinical guidelines" for the treatment of ADHD, seizure disorder, anxiety disorders, depression, reading disabilities, and addictive disorders. The authors state "this suggests that EEG biofeedback should always be considered as an intervention for these disorders" (Hirshberg, Chiu, & Frazier, 2005). The 2009 meta-analysis reviewed studies using neurofeedback only with ADHD. The researchers determined that neurofeedback qualified for an efficacy rating of Level 5 ("efficacious and specific") for ADHD. More precisely, the authors concluded that neurofeedback had the greatest effectiveness on symptoms of inattention and impulsivity and good effectiveness on hyperactivity (Arns, de Ridder, Strehl, Breteler, & Coenen, 2009).

To humanize the research, I'd like to share some real-world examples of neurofeedback success stories from my clinic. A.J. was a struggling student at a local middle school. He had tremendous difficulty focusing in class, often forgot to turn in homework assignments he had actually completed, and was on the verge of failing several subjects. Not surprisingly, he disliked school because he felt like a failure. He was insecure and socially withdrawn.

After three months of consistent neurofeedback training, however, things changed. His parents noticed that he finished his homework much more quickly, with less wailing and gnashing of teeth. He also remembered to turn in his completed assignments. Consequently, his grades went from Fs and Ds to several Bs and an A. His improvement was so dramatic that faculty at his school now recommend neurofeedback to parents before medication.

R.B. was a child who was given a diagnosis of high-functioning autism due to her sensory integration problems; her disruptive, self-soothing behaviors such as spinning and rocking; and her tendency to hyper-focus on a narrow range of interests. She would talk incessantly about topics that were so boring that other students actively avoided her. Moreover, she annoyed them with her disruptive behaviors in the classroom. Although she was bright and sweet-natured, her only friends were adults because her peers could not tolerate her behaviors.

After neurofeedback training, she was able to sit still and focus during class. She also broadened her interests and was able to converse about topics that were interesting to her classmates. She went from never being invited to classmates' birthday parties to getting invited to sleepovers.

Finally, colleagues at my clinic have worked with many adopted children who were abused and neglected in horrible ways before joining their new families. In several cases, the adoptive parents were actually afraid of their adopted kids because the children's behaviors were so unpredictable and potentially violent. Parents had locks installed on their bedroom doors so they could feel safe enough to sleep at night.

None of these children were bad. They were traumatized in ways that no human or animal should ever have to experience. Subsequently, their internal alarm bells were constantly ringing, which resulted in a "kill or be killed" sensibility.

This was brought home to me in a very experiential way. One night I was awakened from a deep sleep when all the smoke detectors in my house began blaring at once. (There was no fire; their batteries had just run too low.) The noise was so loud that it was physically painful. I couldn't focus well enough to think clearly, but all I wanted to do was figure out a way to make the noise stop. Even after removing the batteries from each of the smoke detectors, the incessant racket continued. My heart was pounding and I felt like screaming in frustration. I finally realized I had to disconnect each of the smoke detectors by flipping their respective power switches in my breaker box. The state of alarm, discomfort, and frustration that I experienced that night made it impossible for me to focus on anything else. I can't imagine anyone expecting me to work a math problem or engage in polite conversation when I was in that state of distress.

Traumatized children can feel like this on the inside all the time, with no effective way of making the alarm bells stop. But fortunately, neurofeedback can help them learn how to quieten their inner smoke detectors. Many of the traumatized children trained with neurofeedback at our clinic have been able to lower the volume of their inner alarm bells to a manageable level. Consequently, their awareness has been freed up to engage with their environment and their family members in a more relaxed, open, and healing way.

For more information about neurofeedback, please refer to *Getting Rid of Ritalin* by Robert W. Hill, PhD, and Eduardo Castro, MD; and *Healing Young Brains: The Neurofeedback Solution* by the same authors. To locate a board-certified neurofeedback provider near you, please check the Biofeedback Certification International Alliance (BCIA) website at www.bcia.org or the International Society for Neurofeedback & Research (ISNR) website at www.isnr.net.

Conclusion

If you thoroughly examine the research (especially studies not funded by pharmaceutical companies), you'll find that there's not much evidence to support treating kids' emotional, cognitive, and behavioral problems with psychotropic medications. In my opinion, the meager benefits reported in the literature do not exceed the potential costs, except perhaps in the most extreme cases.

Surely, we can find better ways of helping our children than simply drugging them and putting them at risk for a lifetime of unwanted side effects, not the least of which are an increased chance of being labeled permanently disabled and identifying themselves as mentally ill. For the good of society as a whole, we need to explore healthier ways of empowering our youth to grow, evolve, and succeed.

Recommended Reading List

More Information on Medications

Bass, A. (2008). *Side Effects: A prosecutor, a whistleblower, and a bestselling antidepressant on trial.* Chapel Hill, NC: Algonquin Books.

Breggin, P. R., & Cohen, D. (1999). *Your drug may be your problem: How and why to stop taking psychiatric drugs.* Reading, MA: Perseus Books.

Glasser, H. (2005). *101 reasons to avoid Ritalin like the plague, including 1 great reason why it's almost always unnecessary.* Tucson, AZ: Nurtured Heart.

Jackson, G. E. (2009). *Drug-induced dementia: A perfect crime.* Bloomington, IN: AuthorHouse.

Whitaker, R. (2010). *Anatomy of an epidemic: Magic bullets, psychiatric drugs, and the astonishing rise of mental illness in America.* New York, NY: Crown.

Parenting Books

Bradley, M. J. (2002). *Yes, your teen is crazy! Loving your kid without losing your mind.* Gig Harbor, WA: Harbor Press.

Cline, F. (2006). *Parenting with love and logic: Teaching children responsibility.* Colorado Springs, CO: Piñon Press.

Glasser, H., & Easley, J. (1998). *Transforming the difficult child: The nurtured heart approach.* Tucson, AZ: Center for the Difficult Child.

Siegel, D. J., & Bryson, T. P. (2011). *The whole-brain child: 12 revolutionary strategies to nurture your child's developing mind.* New York, NY: Delacorte Press.

Siegel, D.J., & Bryson, T.P. (2014). *No drama discipline: The whole brain way to calm the chaos and nurture your child's developing mind.* New York, NY: Bantom Books.

Dietary Resources

Compart, P. J., & Laake, D. G. (2009). *The kid-friendly ADHD & autism cookbook: The ultimate guide to the gluten-free, casein-free diet.* Beverly, MA: Fair Winds.

Living Without's gluten-free & more: The magazine for people with allergies and food sensitivities. http://www.glutenfreeandmore.com.

Publications International, Ltd. (2011). *Recipes for gluten-free kids: Fun eats from breakfast to treats!* Lincolnwood, IL: Publications International.

EEG and Neurofeedback

Hill, R. W., & Castro, E. (2002). *Getting Rid of Ritalin: How Neurofeedback Can Successfully Treat Attention Deficit Disorder without Drugs.* Charlottesville, VA: Hampton Roads.

Hill, R. W., & Castro, E. (2009). *Healing Young Brains: The Neurofeedback Solution.* Newburyport, VA: Hampton Roads.

Institute for Applied Neuroscience. http://www.ian-asheville.com.

International Society for Neurofeedback & Research. http://www.isnr.org.

References

Amen, D. G. (2013). *Healing ADD: The breakthrough program that allows you to see and heal the seven types of attention deficit disorder* (Rev. ed.) New York, NY: Penguin.

American Psychiatric Association (APA). (1994). *Diagnostic and statistical manual of mental disorders* (4th ed.). Washington, DC: American Psychiatric Association.

Arns, M., de Ridder, S., Strehl, U., Breteler, M., & Coenen, A. (2009). Efficacy of neurofeedback treatment in ADHD: The effects of inattention, impulsivity, and hyperactivity; A meta-analysis. *Clinical EEG and Neuroscience 40*(3), 180–189.

Arns, M., Feddema, I., & Kenemans, J. L. (2014). Differential effects of theta/beta and SMR neurofeedback in ADHD on sleep onset latency. *Frontiers in Human Neuroscience 8,* 1–10. doi:10.3389/fnhum.2014.01019.

Arns, M., Van der Heijden, K. B., Arnold, L. E., & Kenemans, J. L. (2013). Geographic variation in the prevalence of attention-deficit/hyperactivity disorder: The sunny perspective. *Biological Psychiatry 74*(8), 585–590. doi:10.1016/j.biopsych.2013.02.010.

Astill, R. G., Van der Heijden, K. B., Van Ijzendoorn, M. H., & Van Someren, E. J. (2012). Sleep, cognition, and behavioral problems in school-age children: A century of research meta-analyzed. *Psychology Bulletin 138* (6), 1109–1138. doi:10.1037/a0028204.

Avigan, M. I., Brinker, A. & Diak, I. L. (2009). Pediatric advisory committee follow-up meeting materials, 1–26. Retrieved from http://www.fda.gov/downloads/AdvisoryCommittees/CommitteesMeetingMaterials/PediatricAdvisoryCommittee/UCM191609.pdf.

Bolaños, C., Barrot, M., Berton, O., Wallace-Black, D. & Nestler, E. J. (2003). Methylphenidate treatment during pre- and periadolescence alters behavioral responses to emotional stimuli at adulthood. *Biological Psychiatry, 54*(12), 1317–1329. doi:10.1016/S0006-3223(03)00570-5.

Bornstein, L., & Bornstein, M. H. (2007). Parenting styles and child social development. In Tremblay, R. E., Barr, R. G., & Peters, R. D. (Eds.), *Encyclopedia on Early Childhood Development* (pp. 1–4). Retrieved from http://www.childencyclopedia.com/documents/BornsteinANGxp.pdf. (website inactive)

Billoti de Gage et al. (2012) Benzodiazepine use and risk of dementia: Prospective population based study. *British Medical Journal, 345, e6231*. Retrieved from http://bmj.com/content/345/bmj.e6231.

Food and Drug Administration (FDA). (2009). Labeling change request letter for antidepressant medications. Retrieved from http://www.fda.gov/Drugs/DrugSafety/InformationbyDrugClass/ucm096352.htm.

Food and Drug Administration (FDA). (2005). Medication guide about using antidepressants in children and teenagers. Retrieved from http://www.fda.gov/downloads/drugs/drugsafety/informationbydrugclass/UCM161646.pdf.

Glasser, H. (2005). *101 reasons to avoid Ritalin like the plague, including 1 great reason why it's almost always unnecessary.* Tucson, AZ: Nurtured Heart.

Halperin, J. M., & Healey, D. M. (2011). The influences of environmental enrichment, cognitive enhancement, and physical exercise on brain development: Can we alter the developmental trajectory of ADHD? *Neuroscience & Biobehavioral Reviews 35*(3) 621–634. doi:10.1016/j.neubiorev.2010.07.006.

Han, J. C., Lawlor, D. A., & Kimm, S. Y. (2010). Childhood obesity. *The Lancet, 375*(9727), 1737–1748. doi:10.1016/S0140-6736(10)60171-7.

Harris, G. (2008, November 18). Use of antipsychotics in children is criticized. *The New York Times.* Retrieved from http://www.nytimes.com/2008/11/19/health/policy/19fda.html.

Harris, G., & Carey, B. (2008, June 8). Researchers fail to reveal full drug pay. *The New York Times.* Retrieved from http://www.nytimes.com/2008/06/08/us/08conflict.html?oref=slogin&_r=0.

Hirshberg, L. M., Chiu, S., & Frazier, J. A. (2005). Emerging brain-based interventions for children and adolescents: Overview and clinical perspective. *Child and Adolescent Psychiatry Clinics of North America 14,* 1-19. doi:10.1016/j.chc.2004.07.011.

Horstman, J. (2012). The social treatment. In *The Scientific American healthy aging brain: The neuroscience of making the most of your mature mind* (pp. 167–174). San Francisco, CA: Jossey Bass Wiley.

Jackson, G. (2009). *Drug induced dementia: A perfect crime.* Bloomington, IN: AuthorHouse.

Labbe, C. (2009). Short-term intensive treatment not likely to improve long-term outcomes for children with ADHD. *National Institute of Mental Health.* Retrieved from http://www.nimh.nih.gov/news/science-news/2009/short-term-intensive-treatment-not-likely-to-improve-long-term-outcomes-for-children-with-adhd.shtml.

Matone, M., Localio, R., Huang, Y. S., dosReis, S., Feudtner, C., & Rubin, D. (2012). The relationship between mental health diagnosis and treatment with second-generation antipsychotics over time: A national study of U.S. Medicaid-enrolled children. *Health Services Research, 47*(5), 1836–1860. doi:10.1111/j.1475-6773.2012.01461.x

Matricciani, L., Olds, T., & Petkov, J. (2012). In search of lost sleep: Secular trends in the sleep time of school-aged children and adolescents. *Sleep Medicine Reviews 16*(3), 203–211. doi:10.1016/j.smrv.2011.03.005.

Molina, B. S., Flory, K., Hinshaw, S. P., Greiner, A. R., Arnold, L. E., Swanson, J. M., . . . Wigal, T. (2007). Delinquent behavior and emerging substance use in the MTA at 36 months: Prevalence, course, and treatment effects. *Journal of the American Academy of Child and Adolescent Psychiatry, 46*(8), 1028–1040.

Moreno, C., Laje, G., Blanco, C., Jiang, H., Schmidt, A.B., & Olfson, M. (2007). National trends in the outpatient diagnosis and treatment of bipolar disorder in youth. *Archives of General Psychiatry, 64*(9), 1032-1039.

MTA Cooperative Group. (1999). A 14-month randomized clinical trial of treatment strategies for attention-deficit/hyperactivity disorder. *Archives of General Psychiatry, 56*(12), 1073–1086. Retrieved from http://archpsyc.jamanetwork.com/article.aspx?articleid=205525.

MTA Cooperative Group. (2007). 3-year follow-up of the NIMH MTA study. *Journal of the American Academy of Child and Adolescent Psychiatry, 46*(8), 989–1002. Retrieved from http://www.ncbi.nlm.nih.gov/pubmed/17667478.

Muench, J., & Hamer, A. M. (2010). Adverse effects of antipsychotic medications. *American Family Physician, 81*(5), 617–622. Retrieved from http://www.aafp.org/afp/2010/0301/p617.html.

Patel, N. C., Crismon, M. L., Hoagwood, K., Johnsrud, M. T., Rascati, K. L., Wilson, J. P., & Jensen, P. S. (2005). Trends in the use of typical and atypical antipsychotics in children and adolescents. [Abstract]. *Journal of the American Academy of Child and Adolescent Psychiatry 44*(6), 548–556.

Powers, R. E. (2008). Understanding the side effects of neuroleptics. *Alabama Council of Community Mental Health Boards*. Retrieved from http://www.accmhb.org/docs/2008Conference/handouts/powers (webpage taken down).

Reinberg, S. (2009, June 10). FDA panel OKs newer antipsychotics for children. *HealthDay News*. Retrieved from http://news.health.com/2009/06/11/fda-panel-oks-newer-antipsychotics-children/.

Sonuga-Barke, E. J., Brandeis, D., Cortese, S., Daley, D., Ferrin, M., Holtmann, M. . . . Sergeant, J. (2013). Nonpharmacological interventions for ADHD: Systematic review and meta-analyses of randomized controlled trials of dietary and psychological treatments. *American Journal of Psychiatry.* Retrieved from http://www.ncbi.nlm.nih.gov/pubmed/23360949.

Stevens, L. J., Kuczek, T, Burgess, J. R., Hurt, E., & Arnold, L. E. (2011). Dietary sensitivities and ADHD symptoms: Thirty-five years of research. *Clinical Pediatrics 50*(4), 279–293. doi:10.1177/0009922810384728.

Stump, E. (2009). This way in: Overmedicating for ADHD? *Neurology Now, 5*(2): 8–9.

Vedantam, S. (2009). Debate over drugs for ADHD reignites. *The Washington Post.* Retrieved from http://www.washingtonpost.com/wp-dyn/content/article/2009/03/26/AR2009032604018.html.

Whitaker, R. (2010). *Anatomy of an epidemic: Magic bullets, psychiatric drugs, and the astonishing rise of mental illness in America.* New York, NY: Crown.

Williams, P. A., Haertel, E. H., Haertel, G. D., & Walberg, H. J. (1982). The impact of leisure-time television on school learning: A research synthesis. *American Educational Research Journal 19*(1), 19–50. doi:10.3102/00028312019001019.

About the Author

Mary Ammerman was born in Nashville, TN, and raised in the foothills of North Carolina. She received her bachelor's degrees in English and psychology from UNC-Chapel Hill and her doctoral degree in clinical psychology from Pepperdine University. She enjoys her work as Vice President of the Institute for Applied Neuroscience, located in beautiful Asheville, NC. She values the gift of human consciousness (her own and others') and intends to make the most of it while she has it. This includes dancing whenever possible.

Made in the USA
Monee, IL
04 November 2026

67387887R00030